The Golden Principles of Personal Finance

Anthony Kennedy

Table of Content

Introduction

Bad money management. It sounds nasty, and you probably want nothing to do with it.

However, a good portion of Americans don't properly manage their money. Some sources report that Americans are pretty bad when it comes to their finances as compared to other developed countries.

There is hope for you if you find yourself in this group.

There are some great tried-and-tested strategies you can learn how to manage your money the right way.

Let's take a look.

Having a sound money management plan can be the light at the end of the tunnel for people trying to get their financial life in order.

If you are like me and have several bank accounts, credit cards, an IRA, and the like, often getting a grip and fully understanding your financial state might seem daunting and an uphill struggle.

But if you don't take the proper steps to get organized and learn ways for better managing your finances, you'll feel like you are swimming against the current.

Managing your money like anything takes time to understand and to improve on. And to master, it also takes commitment and a solid understanding of your financial situation. These are the first steps in effective money management.

Everyone and anyone who ever took control of their finances went through this; and getting your financial life in order, sooner rather than later, is of utmost importance.

What Is Personal Finance?

Personal finance is that the money management that a private or an extended family performs to budget, save, and pay financial resources over time, taking into consideration various financial risks and future life events. Once designing personal finances, the individual would consider the quality of his or her wants of a spread of banking merchandise (checking, savings accounts, credit cards and client loans) or investment personal equity, (stock market, bonds, mutual funds) and insurance (life insurance, insurance, incapacity insurance) merchandise or participation and observance of and- or employer-sponsored retirement plans, social security benefits, and income tax management. Before a specialty in personal finance was developed, various disciplines which are closely related to it, such as family economics, and client political economy were instructed in different faculties as a part of household arts for over one hundred years. The earliest best-known analysis in personal finance was wiped out 1920 by Hazel Kyrk. Her thesis at the University of Chicago set the inspiration of client political economy and family political economy.

Margaret Reid, an academic of household arts at Same University, is recognized united of the pioneers within the study of client behavior and house behavior.

Are you struggling with your finances regardless of how much money you earn? Are you having a hard time knowing how to manage money effectively?

Whether you earn $2,000, $4,000 or $8,000 a month or more, you struggle to pay for your bills and barely have enough money to save. Sometimes, you even think about asking for a raise, getting a second job or an extra freelance work so you could make ends meet. Then you realize people are earning less than you that are doing much better with their finances than you are.

How Could That Be?

The reality is that it doesn't matter how much you earn. Managing money is a responsibility, and if you can't manage $1,000 effectively, you can't expect to manage $1,000,000, either. You have to be able to handle the small ones first before you can take on bigger, more challenging tasks.

Why Is It Important To Learn How To Manage Your Money?

Think of money as a person.

If you treat someone poorly, you don't give them the respect they deserve, and you take them for granted, would that person stay? Chances are they won't.

On the other hand, if you value a person, you take care of them. You do absolutely everything necessary to make them stay and keep them from leaving you.

If you badly want to get out of debt or if you want to build a fortune and provide a better life for your family, you have to learn how to use money to your advantage instead of letting money take control over you.

Importance of Managing Personal Finances

Managing your finances doesn't have to be complicated.

Young, motivated and tech-savvy adults have all the information you need to manage your finances right at your fingertips. Managing your money is probably one of the single most important accomplishments you can achieve. Every aspect of your life depends on it.

Unlimited Career Options

Even though your education or credentials make you an ideal candidate for your first job, managing your finances may determine how far you'll go in your career. The number of employers who use credit checks is increasing.

"Recent statistics are scarce, but when the Society for Human Resource Management polled its members in 2006, 43 percent of their companies ran credit checks on some or all potential hires," MSN Money contributor Liz Pulliam Weston reports.

Employers are using background investigations -- and credit checks -- to determine who's best qualified for a job or promotion. If it comes down to two equally qualified candidates, the one who demonstrates she's managed her finances well might be picked over somebody who hasn't.

Less Stress

The stress of having your finances out of whack can take its toll on your body and mind. Managing your finances can be as important to your physical and mental health as working out at the gym. Stress has a way of affecting every part of your life.

Take control of your finances from this point forward and work out problems as quickly as they arise. However, don't become so obsessed with finances and money to the point where you can't enjoy yourself. Make wise decisions about spending and saving.

Lower Interest Rates

Buying your first home is a big step. Managing your finances is important for a few reasons when it comes to getting the biggest bang for your buck. When you have control of your finances, you can qualify for lower interest rates on a home, which means you can pay less for your home and still enjoy your own space. Another advantage of managing your finances is that you can sleep well at night knowing you can make a mortgage payment that doesn't make you "house poor." House poor means you spend all of your money -- income and discretionary cash -- on your home.

If you manage your finances well, you can save enough for a sizable down payment, which can reduce your monthly payments even more. You also can afford to make extra payments on your mortgage each year, creating a faster track to a mortgage-free lifestyle.

Enjoy an Early Retirement

For young adults, retirement planning sounds like a far away and distant goal. However, if you manage your finances well, you could be sipping margaritas on a tropical island or traveling the globe while you're still young enough to enjoy an active lifestyle.

Once you're working and saving toward retirement, talk to friends and mentors about your long-range goals.

Bouncing ideas off others can help. Even if you want to work until the traditional retirement age, managing your finances is important for lots of reasons. You might want to start a family someday. Having an investment plan in addition to your retirement savings is a smart way to go.

How Do Millionaires Handle Their Money?

According to T. Harv Eker, one thing that's similar between all millionaires (and billionaires for that matter) is that they all manage their money very well.

With enough practice, anyone can master how to manage money effectively. It is simple yet valuable concept shared by T. Harv Eker in his book (The secrets of the Millionaire mind) is pretty helpful when it comes to keeping your finances in order. It's called the jars concept and here's how it works:

Whatever amount of money you earn (net, minus the tax), divide it into 6 jars or bank accounts if you like.

• 10% of your money goes to your FFA (financial freedom account)

• 10% to LTSS (long-term savings for spending)

• 10% to your educational account

• 55% to your utilities

• 10% to your fun account

• 5% to your give account

So, let's say you earned $3,000 net for the month. This is how you should divide your money:

• FFA – $300

• Education – $300

• LTSS – $300

• Utilities – $1,650

• Fun – $300

• Give – $150

If you are married and you have a common bank account, you can combine your money and divide the total amount into the jars.

It doesn't matter if one person is earning more than the other. Keep in mind that in a relationship, money is just one aspect.

The amount of money you're budgeting is not important, too. What matters is that you get into the habit of managing your money. This way, as your capacity to earn money grows, so does the money that you put in the jars.

How Do The Jars Work?

FFA (Financial Freedom Account)

People like to call this a savings account, but we like to call it the FFA. Why? This is not just your savings. It's your golden goose.

This is the first account you should put money in because this will set you up for financial freedom.

The money that goes into this account will only be used if you're going to spend it on something that's going to make you money.

And since this is your golden goose, you don't want to kill it. If you are going to invest money from this account, make sure not to use it all up.

Long-Term Savings for Spending (LTSS)

This jar works in a variety of ways.

We use the money in this jar to pay for things we want to buy but might need to save for first. It can be a house, vacation or a new car.

In case you are in debt, use the money in this jar to pay it off.

If you want to get over your debt, shift your mindset into thinking of ways to make money and your debt will be paid off.

You can also use this account if an unexpected expense arises. Let's say you got invited to a birthday and need to buy a gift; you can take money from this jar.

Education Account

The most successful people are the ones who continue learning, so it is important that you invest in your continued education, too.

For context, Warren Buffet claims to read 500 pages a day. It's not a coincidence that he's one of the richest men in the world.

If you want to learn a new skill, go ahead and attend that seminar you always wanted to go to. Buy that book that might help you improve your mindset. Use this money if you want to go back to school.

The money from this account is to improve your skills and knowledge.

Utility Jar

This is also known as your budget. This is where you get money to pay for your rent, house mortgage, car loans, and other bills.

Now, sticking to the example salary above, let's say you're on a $3000 paycheck and are supposed to allocate $1650 to pay for your utilities. You might be saying, "That's too little" or" It's not enough." This is the part where you have to learn to be creative and think of ways to save money or think of the bills that have to go.

For example, if you're paying for a monthly gym membership of $50 which you don't frequently go to, it's a good idea to cancel that membership. Find an alternative activity that might not cost as much. This can be biking, yoga or hiking.

If you're paying for Netflix but are not watching anyway, cancel it.

Fun Account

The key to living a happy life is balance in everything.

So, if you are saving all this money to invest in the future, it's just fair that you enjoy your money as well.

Use the money in this account to go to that nice restaurant or get a massage.

Blow the money and leave nothing. If you want, you can save the money in your fun account for up to 3 months.

However, if this account is already empty and you still want to have a good time or there are still things you want to buy, do not take money from the other accounts to satisfy your urge.

Don't borrow money and don't take our your credit card. It only means that you cannot afford it anymore. You either have to save for it first, or you can think of ways to make more money.

Give account

It also sends a signal to your brain and the universe that money is abundant in this world, that there is more than enough for you. When you send signals like that to the universe.

If you want to take it a step further, give something that is more important than money. You can choose to give your time as well. Giving money is great but giving your time is just as valuable.

The Golden Rules Of Personal Finance

Managing your finances feels like nothing but a lot of paperwork and numbers. You make X amount of dollars, you spend Y amount, and you try to make sure Y is less than X. However, your finances are just as much about psychology, habits, and the values you choose to live by. Put another way, your mindset matters as much as math.

Beneath all the software and the budgets, there are a few rules that will always help improve your financial life:

• Spend less money than you earn: If you earn $30,000/year and you spend $31,000/year, you'll end up in a spiral of debt that's hard to walk away from. If you spend exactly as much as you earn every year, you'll never be prepared for emergencies or major life changes. Spending less than you earn allows you the freedom to save, to prepare for the future, and deal with the inevitable crises that life throws at you. The bigger the gap between your income and your spending, the better.

• Always plan for the future: This doesn't just mean retirement. When a store offers to let you pay off some gadget in 6 months with no interest, you need to know you can pay it off, or avoid that deal. Establishing an emergency fund will allow you to deal with unexpected car repairs or medical bills. Having a retirement plan will ensure you have income when you're unable to work anymore. Your finances should always look forward beyond the current month.

• Make your money make more money: Want to know how the rich keep getting richer? It's because money can grow while you sleep, provided you save some of it. Properly invested money earns more money over time. Don't just sock all your cash away in a low-interest savings account. Invest in things that will earn you more money than you had before. Sometimes that's an investment account, but sometimes it's starting a business, or even getting an education to get a better paying job.

The most important personal finance rules don't change. What your grandparents did may not work for you. There will always be newer, better tools to manage your money. However, spending less than you earn will always be beneficial. Investing your money will always be better than doing nothing with it. And planning for the future will always be better than blowing your paycheck as soon as you get it.

How To Create And Manage A Budget

Budgeting has a bad reputation among a lot of America households who view it as a way to strip all the fun out of spending money. No more shopping. No more eating out at restaurants. No more golfing on weekends.

A budget shows merely how much money you have coming in and how those funds are spent. It's one of the most important tools in building a successful financial future because it helps you get the most out of your money.

Regardless of economic standing or which generation you fall into, every consumer can benefit from creating and managing a budget. A budget gives people a sense of control over their money. Think of a budget as a financial foundation. Each person's foundation is going to be different, just as each financial situation is different.

Choosing A Budgeting System

There are four basic ways to create, track and monitor a budget. Each system uses different techniques, but they all center on organization and attention to detail.

• **The Notebook and Pen:** This is the oldest method for budgeting, and it's also the least expensive option. With this method, you write down all your sources of income and all your expenses. If they balance, you're good to go.

• **The Spreadsheet:** The most popular spreadsheet software for budgeting is Microsoft Excel. Many websites offer free samples of Excel budgeting worksheets that consumers can use, instead of trying to create their own. A spreadsheet lets you organize a lot of information easily and does the math for you.

• **Free Online Software:** Several free web-based software programs can help with budgeting. Such programs like Manilla and Mint.com allow you to create and group your expenses into categories and track your spending, so you can see exactly where your money is going as soon as the transaction takes place.

• **Financial Software:** There are also financial software programs, but you need to be computer-savvy to use them. Quicken is a leading product.

• **Dave Ramsey's Zero-Based Budgeting:** Popular financial personality Dave Ramsey recommends a zero-based budgeting system where you pre-assign all of your dollars at the beginning of the month using envelopes.

You can also check with your local credit union or bank for tips and tricks. Your saving institution may even have budgeting worksheets on hand to get you started. If you prefer, the U.S. Financial Literacy and Education Commission (FLEC) has numerous budgeting worksheets and resources to help you at any stage of life.

Creating a Budget

Budgeting strategies and techniques vary across the board. There will be differences, for example, between what works for a first-year college student and one for a retiree. But there are five necessary steps in creating a budget. They are all important because they build on one another, helping you organize your finances sensibly.

Step 1: Set Goals

There are two types of financial goals: immediate and long range. Immediate goals focus on using your money today, while long-range goals deal with saving and spending over decades. Both are important, and complement one another: Saving money today affects what you spend now but also how much you'll have later in life.

You need to determine which goals address necessities and which ones cover luxuries. Then, you can prioritize your financial goals accordingly.

Immediate financial goals include covering current expenses. Some of these are obligatory and include your mortgage or rent payment, car loans, utility bills, child care, food, cell phone, and household supplies. Secondary goals, called discretionary items, include non-essential clothing, subscriptions, dining out and taking vacations. Long-range financial goals could also include retirement savings, investments, and charitable donations. If you have debt, paying it down can be both obligatory and discretionary. Making required payments is essential to financial solvency, but paying debt early, while not required, can make long-term sense.

Step 2: Calculate Your Income and Expenses

After you determine your financial goals, you need a plan for reaching them. To do this, you need to evaluate your income and your expenses. Most people budget monthly because most bills follow a monthly schedule.

Start by making a list of your monthly income sources, including your salary (after taxes), any bonuses you incur regularly, and child support or alimony payments. If you don't know the exact amount, you can use an estimate. Once you have your numbers, add them up. The total is your monthly income.

The next part of the equation is your expenses, which fall into three categories: fixed costs committed, committed variable expenditures, and discretionary expenses.

• Fixed committed expenses: These have a fixed monthly amount, such as your mortgage or rent.

• Variable committed expense: These vary from one month to the next month based on need and would include groceries and gasoline.

• Discretionary expenses: As noted, these are optional expenses and include recreation and entertainment. A gym membership would also fall into this category. Discretionary expenses often make life more fulfilling, but they should be the first expenses to go if you can't afford the basics.

If you fail to pay off your credit card bills each month, you'll begin to pay a great deal of interest. This can play havoc with any budget. If your carried-over credit card payments eat up more than 10% of your monthly income, you should consider speaking with a nonprofit credit counselor. Over the telephone or online, a free credit counseling session will walk you through your budget and recommend expenses that can be reduced or eliminated. If you qualify for a debt management program, you may be able to reduce your monthly debt payments as well.

Step 3: Analyze Your Spending and Balance Your Checkbook

The goal in budgeting is to make sure your expenses do not exceed your income. If they do, and more money is going out than is coming in, then you need to make adjustments. This doesn't necessarily mean you need to start penny-pinching; it just means it is time to revisit the discretionary cost category and see where you are willing and able to cut the fat.

If you make any payments by check, your checkbook register can help you keep track of incoming and outgoing money, and what you spend money on. Although paying by check is becoming rarer, those who stick to this payment method should keep their checkbooks balanced. This will help you avoid overdraft fees or bounced checks, and it can shed some light on your spending habits.

Here are the basics:

• Keep records for all your deposits and purchases. Record each one in your check register, which the bank will provide you.

• Print out or download your monthly bank statement if you aren't already getting one in the mail. If you're doing everything online, there is software that can make this step — and budgeting — easy.

• Do your math for deposits and withdrawals to make sure your bank hasn't missed anything or taken liberties with your money. Reconcile line by line, making sure your record of checks is the same as the statement.

• Find the ending number from each monthly statement and work backward, check to see what has cleared, and what has not cleared. Deposits that haven't cleared will need to be subtracted from your balance. If your checks haven't cleared, they will have to be added back to your balance until they do.

• Go line by line and account for any fees you're charged. Seeing them up close may prompt you to call and ask to have some removed, which the banks often will do if you persist. Also, add the pennies of interest you may have received.

• Again, if you have access to a computer or even a smartphone, this process can be automated using financial software or apps, saving you time and frustration. The goal is to review your cash flow, look for errors and learn from what you see.

Step 4: Revisit Your Original Budget

After you've had a chance to monitor your income and expenses for a month or two, you will be more aware of areas that need adjusting. Maybe your initial monthly income estimates were off, or perhaps you didn't account for expenses like car repairs or veterinary bills. Make adjustments, but always balance inflows with outflows.

Once you work out all the kinks in your budget, you need to commit to following it. No budget is forever, however, so periodic reviews are key to success.

If you get a promotion, for example, you can increase your discretionary spending as well as your savings goals. On the other hand, a layoff or fewer work hours could mean cutting back on spending until you restore your income.

Savings should be part of the plan. Financial planners recommend that your savings cover six months of income, enough to compensate for a job loss or other emergency. You might find it useful to open a separate savings account and fund it gradually until you reach the goal. Keeping a separate account will make it more difficult to raid the emergency fund to cover non-essentials.

Step 5: Commitment

Creating a budget is a great step in working toward a more financially sound future for you and your family. Committing to your budget will get you there. Remain realistic, evaluate it often and don't be afraid to adjust. Budgeting is all about balance.

Managing Your Budget When Unexpected Bills Arrive

As mentioned, an emergency fund is crucial to financial security. Start by setting aside $50 per week. In a year, you would have $2,600, plus any interest, for when the refrigerator stops working or when the transmission blows.

Experts recommend looking at your withholding taxes to find hidden cash. If you receive a large refund every year, perhaps you need to change your filing status to receive additional money in your paycheck to put toward an emergency fund. Unless that is, you are putting your tax return funds into that fund.

Medical crises, in particular, can turn a balanced budget upside down. Negotiate large medical expenses, such as an emergency hospital stay, with the hospital. Almost all hospitals negotiate fees. Often if you contact them immediately instead of waiting until the amount goes into collections, the hospital or provider's office can set up a payment plan.

If not, a medical bill consolidation may help, as it allows you to combine all your medical bills into one lower monthly bill through an agency or a bank loan. This not only makes it easier on you, but the arrangement protects your credit score because you can make on-time payments. The downside is it may take you longer to pay your debt in full.

Benefits Of Budgeting

Everyone can benefit from taking a transparent and proactive approach to controlling their finances. Committing to your budget will help guide you into a much better financial position.

Budgeting can improve your life because of it:

• Reveals waste. Creating a budget sheds light on areas that many people neglect on a day-to-day basis.

• Directs priorities. A budget allows for people to look at the big picture of their spending habits and set new priorities to maximize their money's potential.

• Creates new habits. When people get a clearer picture of how they've been using their money, it allows them to shift expenditures into different categories, making them more conscious of unnecessary spending.

• Reduces stress. Finances are one of the top stress-inducing situations. When there is a sense of control over the money coming in and the money going out, the stress can transform into a feeling of empowerment.

• Educates. Having a budget allows people to view money as a tool, shifting the mindset to focus on long-term goals and future needs.

Creating a budget is the first step, but maintaining the budget is where you start to see real growth in yourself and more stretch in your dollar. Sticking to a budget can be a difficult task for people who aren't used to spending boundaries or self-discipline in their finances, so it's important to maintain a positive attitude toward the process.

Staying motivated can help alleviate some of the pressures of budgeting. Consider setting aside some money each month so you can look forward to a relaxing vacation at the end of the year.

Finally, set realistic goals. Start slowly, building up to a plan that works for you and your lifestyle.

The Finer Points

Wants vs. Needs

"You Can't Always Get What You Want," one of the Rolling Stones popular 1960s hits, touches on an issue many of us face all the time. The message is you might not be able to get things you want, but if you try, you'll get what you need.

How do you separate wants from needs and why bother? For many of us, knowing where to draw the line can mean the difference between creating a successful budget and going broke. So what's the difference. Most needs are synonymous with non-discretionary expenditures. They include shelter, which demands payment of rent or a mortgage, and food, which results in grocery bills. There are plenty of other items that are basic and non-negotiable, but the non-negotiable category leaves room for choice.

For instance, if you need a car to get to work, you could buy a used Kia sedan or a new BMW. The price difference is huge, and the Beemer is certain to impress your friends and offer a fine driving experience. The question is what you can afford? If you make a $500,000 a year, the BMW might be yours without stretching your finances. But if you're taking home $40,000, it's better to stick with the Kia.

The same rule applies to house – should you rent a one-bedroom apartment or buy a $400,000 house? Again, both offer shelter, but at radically different costs.

There's also the difference between needs and items that you could get by without. Think about taking a vacation to Thailand versus a week driving to state parks near your home. Both can offer satisfying and relaxing places to spend your downtown, but the costs are radically different. Also, think about impulse buys. Say you go to home improvement store to buy some lawn fertilizer and leave with a lawnmower you hadn't planned to buy. You might need a new mover, but it's a good idea to research models and prices before putting your money down.

Knowing the difference between wants and needs is key to a successful budget. You can budget for some impulse purchases or product upgrades, but understand what you're doing, show restraint and always make sure your budget balances.

Seasonal Expenses

A sizable amount of your money is likely to go to one-off expenses that arise throughout a year. Examples include holiday presents, birthday gifts, summer vacation costs, and back-to-school spending. Some seasonal expenses are for stand-alone items like presents, others are for basics. Heating your home is an issue for the cold-weather months, for instance, and a higher water bill might coincide with irrigating your lawn in the summer. Clothing is also seasonal, with swimming suits for the summer and heavy jackets for the winter.

When you draw a budget, study your outflows during the past year or two and estimate the impact of annual costs, then build those costs into your plan. If your summer costs are much higher than springtime, make sure you save enough in the spring to fund spending in the summer.

Checking in on Your Budget

Budgets are living documents. Just as life is continually changing, the demands on your budget change too. For that reason, it's good to regularly review your budget to adjust for changes in income and expenses.

What should you consider? On the income side, you should make adjustments if you get a raise or receive a windfall like an inheritance. You need to adjust if you lose your job or move to a new one. Getting married or divorced requires a massive reworking of your budget. So does having a child. Sometimes the changes are smaller or temporary, things like a medical insurance copayment might require a temporary adjustment.

You don't need to overhaul your entire budget when changes happen. Your rent is rent, and what you spend each month on your car is unlikely to change. But other things are more flexible. If your income drops, you might eat out less. If it goes up, you could save more, pay off debt quicker or make a discretionary purchase.

There's no hard and fast rule about when to review your budget. Some financial consultants suggest doing it regularly. Others suggest every several months. It's probably good to consider revisiting your budget when life-changing events occur and set intervals to adjust for smaller stuff like inflation and changes in fixed costs.

Automatic Saving and Recommended Percentages

You should strongly consider making automatic saving a part of your budget. What is automatic saving? It's the money you set aside for funding an emergency account, paying for Christmas gifts later in the year or creating a college fund for your kids.

Automatic saving is best handled through paycheck withholding. If you're saving for retirement and your company offers a 401(k) plan, sign up and have money withheld from your paycheck. Many employers also offer medical and childcare savings plans, which are typically tax exempt. You can also have your salary automatically deposited in a checking account, then transfer part of the pay to a savings account that you don't plan to touch.

There are many strategies for automatic savings. Talk to a financial adviser to learn more about the options and what amount of saving you can afford. Once you implement a plan, stick with it. Percentages will vary, but if your company matches contributions to your 401(k), save at least the maximum amount that will be matched. Other savings will be largely determined by your income and expenses. If you need to withhold 20% of your paycheck to cover the rent, make sure you do it. Knowing how much money you need and saving for it will make sure you meet your expenses and prepare for the future.

Financial experts have come up with the recommended percentages for spending to help people budgeting for the first time. For example, it is suggested you spend no more than 30% of your gross monthly income on housing, whether you're renting or owning.

Automobiles are the next biggest expense for consumers and probably the biggest temptation to overspend. The best idea is to keep spending between 10% and 15% of your monthly income. Anything beyond that stretches you thin, especially if a financial emergency arises.

Student loans might be another variable in your monthly budget. Several income-based repayment plans limit your payments to 10-15% of your income. That's a safe number, but often will extend payments a few years and end up costing you a small fortune in interest charges. Try using 20% of your budget, especially if you don't have a car payment or are splitting rent with roommates.

Other suggested percentages for ongoing expenses include utilities (10%); food (10-15%) and savings (10-15%).

Timing Your Budget

You should commit to staying on the budget until you see results. The best way to accomplish this is to create an annual plan that covers your fixed costs like rent and car payment, your annual costs like holiday presents and vacations and your discretionary costs like eating out and buying clothes. Work all these things into a 12-month projection and follow it.

If you find flaws in the plan or your cash flow changes, you can modify it. Otherwise, try to stay with it. Consider using budgeting software or apps to help you. If you discipline yourself, you'll be surprised as debts get paid, savings grow, and your needs are met.

Ways You Can Learn How To Manage Your Finances More Simply.

Of course, there are many other ways you can simplify your financial life.

You can learn how to manage your finances effectively by taking part in the actions below to make your life more simple:

• Start a cash budget. Dealing with only cash would be very easy as you won't ever have to worry about making a credit card payment.

• Get rid of credit cards or slim down. If you are not interested in credit card rewards, then slimming down to just one credit card can save a lot of hassle and time.

• Pay off your loans. Whether you have student loan debt, credit card debt, car debt, or whatever else, paying it off will help manage your finances easier as you will have less debt causing you stress.

• Create a budget through Excel. This can save you time in that you can easily make changes whenever they need to be made. It's not as easy to make changes or have a flexible budget when you write it down as eventually, it would turn into one sloppy mess.

• Opt for paying expenses annually or semiannually. Instead of paying for bills like home insurance and car insurance monthly, you might want to look into paying it every six months or once a year. You will probably qualify for a discount if you do this as well. That's two fewer bills to worry about each month if you do this!

• Cut expenses out of your life. Each one you cut out means one less bill to worry about and money saved.

The Best Tools For Learning How To Manage Money

Learning how to manage money is an important life skill, and there have never been more accessible resources to teach people how to manage money, invest and plan for the future. Indeed the market is flooded; an overwhelming number of books, blogs, apps, podcasts, etc. that give their audience free financial information is impossible to sift through, there just are not enough hours in the day. But knowing the fundamentals of finance: how to manage loans, debt, budgets, mortgages, insurance, investing, etc. will facilitate your future. So to save some time, here are the best free resources for a personal financial education:

1. Mint.com

One of the most accessible and most popular personal finance tools available, and it is excellent. Mint is free, it is easy and helps you maintain the budget you set by sending you notifications when you've hit a certain budget for the month. It enables you to maintain the good financial habits you want to start forming now. It is one of the best tools on the market that gives you a great overlook of your financial health.

2. Learnvest

In the interest of full disclosure, LearnVest is a fellow Forbes contributor. But it is a wonderful, helpful resource, and considered to be a personal finance 101 of sorts. Whether you want to know more about earning, saving, budgeting, taxes, mortgages, investing, etc. It is a great resource whether you are just learning about money, or you are trying to deepen your understanding of it.

3. The Simple Dollar

This blog is a resource of 101 courses in investing, banking, loans, insurance, credit, etc. It's a great starting point for making well-informed and strategic investment decisions.

4. Robinhood App

The Robinhood app is a straightforward brokerage service app designed for mobile phones that offers free trading and geared toward beginning investors. The app makes investing in certain stocks very easy for millennials. It profits from the accrued interest of clients' uninvested cash balances.

5. Stacking Benjamins Podcast

This podcast gets more in-depth about particular topics such as paying off debt, investing in real estate, strategies for finding more time and money, even an amusement park savings guide. It also focuses on building wealth and creating multiple income streams.

6. So Money Podcast

Journalist, author and personal finance expert Farnoosh Torabi interviews entrepreneurs and thought leaders about building their respective businesses, personal finance and their personal experiences with money.

7. The Tim Ferriss Show Podcast

A top-rated podcast for years, Ferriss interviews celebrities, intellects, and entrepreneurs to discuss their tactics and routines, including favorite philosophies, books, morning routines, exercise regimens, time-management strategies and more that have contributed to their financial and personal success.

Saving For The Future

So, you've started budgeting your money, you're building credit, and you're spending less than you earn. Maybe it took you a couple of months, but you're finally in control of your finances. Great! Now comes the next part: saving for the future. Maybe it seems too far away to matter, or maybe it feels impossible and overwhelming. However, the earlier you start saving, the more money you'll have later on in life—and the less effort you'll spend trying to get there later on.

To start with, you remember those sections in your budget that you made earlier called Savings and Investments? Start by saving those automatically. If your employer uses direct deposit (which means your money goes directly to your bank account, rather than giving you a check you can cash), you can ask to have a portion of your pay sent to multiple accounts. You can use this to send money to a separate savings account that you don't have a debit card for, or that's not easy to transfer to your regular checking account. The money you never have access to is the easiest to save. Even if you can't set aside whole chunks of your paycheck, services like Acorns can round up your everyday purchases to the nearest dollar and automatically save the difference.

Having your money in a savings account will help you save for little things, like your emergency fund or a new computer. But your real, long-term savings are going toward something far more important: retirement. Yes, one day, you'll want to stop working, and you'll need a big chunk of savings to keep you going in your golden years, and a little savings account isn't the best way to do that. That's where investments come in. If you can put your savings into some relatively simple, low-risk investments, it'll make money for you while you sleep— and throughout years and decades, that can add up to an awful lot. This is how you save enough to retire one day.

Investing doesn't have to be complicated, either—it doesn't mean picking winning stocks or timing the market. If you're starting, you can use a "robot-advisor" service like Betterment or Wealthfront to do it all automatically for you. It'll guide you through the process of setting up an investment plan based on your age, goals, and risk preferences. It will then automatically pick which companies or industries to invest in. If you want to get more hands-on, we detail more tools for managing your investments here.

Long-term investments can also come from your employer. Many companies offer 401(k)s that you can fund with money deducted from your paycheck before taxes. In many cases, employers will also match how much you contribute, which means you're getting free money just for having an investment account with them. If your employer offers a 401(k) contribution, it's advisable that you at least contribute as much as your employer will match.

Getting started with long-term investments will often be one of the hardest parts of your financial life because, when you're just starting, you don't have much money. For that reason, it's important that you re-examine your investments every time you get a raise or a new job that pays you more. When you make more money, it's tempting to upgrade your life with a new car, apartment, or expensive toys to match your new budget. This is what's called "lifestyle inflation." While it's okay to move up, you'll also never have a better time to boost your long-term savings than when you're already living on a smaller budget than you're earning.

Conclusion

If you feel you have a better understanding of your income and have a budget that covers your expenses, you have succeeded in taking control of your finances. But some people want to take the additional step of making their money work for them (earning money off of their money.) This can be a fun and rewarding process, but it can also be complicated and risky. Not all types of investments are guaranteed to make you money - sometimes you can lose the money you already have.

Everyone aspires to achieve a good quality of life for themselves and their families. This invariably means getting the very most out of your finances. You should be aware that however well you manage your finances while in service you are, as a part of your terms and conditions of service, benefitting from being subsidized in certain areas which means you will lose these benefits resulting in higher costs when you leave the Service. Subsidies include; food and accommodation, some social and leisure activities, sport, fitness facilities, travel/commuting, child care facilities, work clothing, professional development training, medical, dental and rehabilitation services and prescription charges.

It is human nature to want nice things and live well. In a society that demands instant fulfillment it requires strength of character and personal discipline to resist these pressures and temptations if they cannot be afforded. Good money management is an important part of achieving your long term goals, success, and happiness. It is a life skill that most learn over time and out of necessity. Adopting this life skill early puts you in control, will increase your opportunities, reduces stress and uncertainty, and promote good health, well-being, and lasting relationships. Money management includes such things as controlling your finances and living within your means, to saving for short and long-term goals, to taking control of your financial situation and having a realistic plan to pay off your debts.